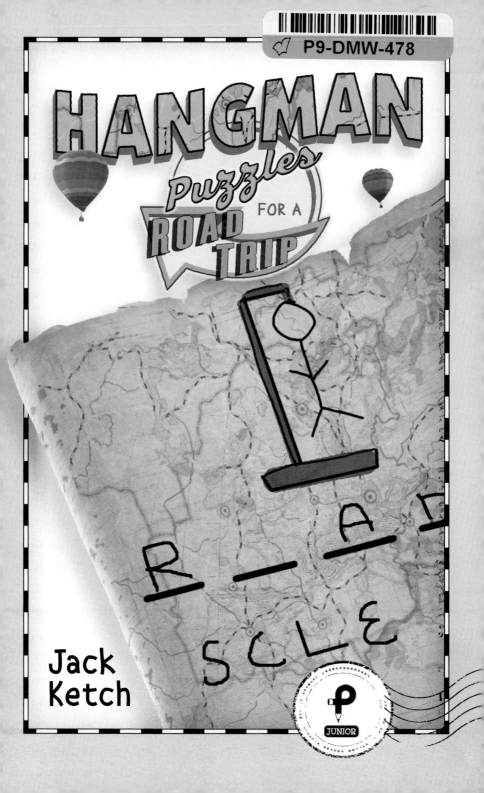

PUZZLE
WRIGHT
JUNIOR

JUNIOR New York

An Imprint of Sterling Publishing Co., Inc.
1166 Avenue of the Americas
New York, NY 10036

ISBN 978-1-4549-3158-4

Distributed in Canada by Sterling Publishing
c/o Canadian Manda Group, 664 Annette Street
Toronto, Ontario M6S 2C8, Canada
Distributed in the United Kingdom by GMC Distribution Services
Castle Place, 166 High Street, Lewes, East Sussex BN7 1XU, England
Distributed in Australia by NewSouth Books, University of New South Wales,
Sydney, NSW 2052, Australia

For information about custom editions, special sales, and premium and
corporate purchases, please contact Sterling Special Sales at 800-805-5489
or specialsales@sterlingpublishing.com.

Manufactured in China
Lot #:
2 4 6 8 10 9 7 5 3 1
02/19

Cover design by Valerie Hou

sterlingpublishing.com
puzzlewright.com

RULES

Hello! You must be very brave, because simply by opening this book you have chosen to play a dangerous game: hangman. Your goal is to reveal a word or phrase by correctly guessing the missing letters before you (represented by the stick figure in the gallows) are hanged. First, pick a letter and scratch off the silver circle beneath it. If that letter is correct, one or more numbers will tell you which blanks you should write that letter in. But if you guess incorrectly, a bold ✖ will be revealed, which means you must draw in one of the stick figure's body parts. (You can draw them in any order; the hangman is generous that way.)

The stick figure's body has six parts: a head, a torso, two arms, and two legs. If you spell the entire word or phrase before the stick figure is completed, you win! If you don't … well, it was nice knowing you. And now, if you're ready, you may turn the page and begin.

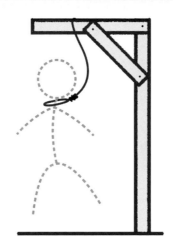

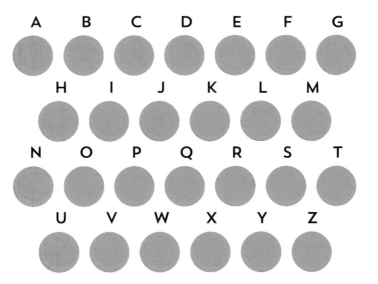

$\overline{}$ $\overline{}$ $\overline{}$ $\overline{}$ $\overline{}$ $\overline{}$ $\overline{}$
1 2 3 4   5 6 7

$\overline{}$ $\overline{}$ $\overline{}$ $\overline{}$ $\overline{}$ $\overline{}$ $\overline{}$ $\overline{}$
8 9 10 11 12 13 14 15

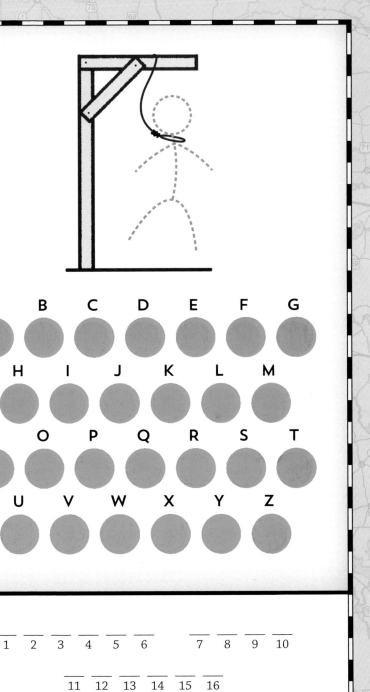

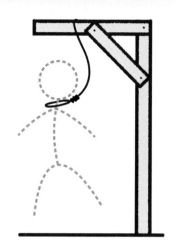

A B C D E F G
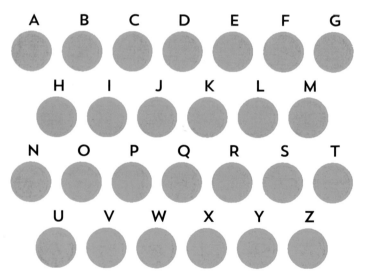
H I J K L M

N O P Q R S T

U V W X Y Z

___ ___ ___ ___   ___ ___ ___ ___
1   2   3   4   5   6   7   8

___ ___ ___   ___ ___ ___ ___ ___ ___ ___
9   10 11   12 13 14 15 16 17 18

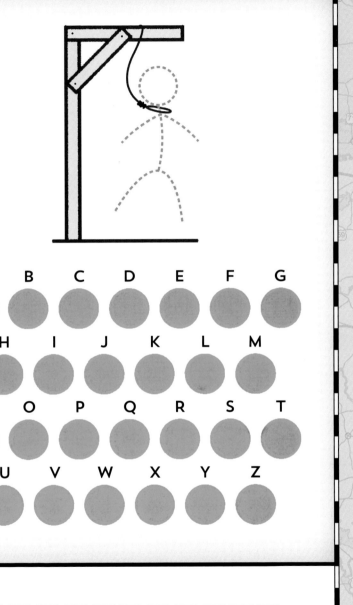

A B C D E F G

H I J K L M

N O P Q R S T

U V W X Y Z

___ ___ ___ ___ ___ ___ ___ ___ ___ ___ ___
1   2   3   4   5   6   7   8   9 10 11

___ ___ ___ ___ ___
12 13 14 15 16

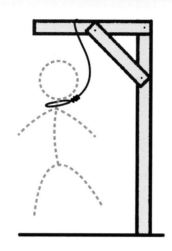

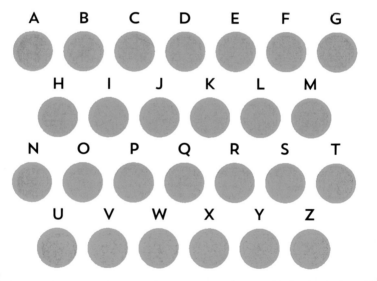

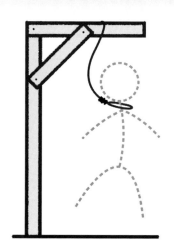

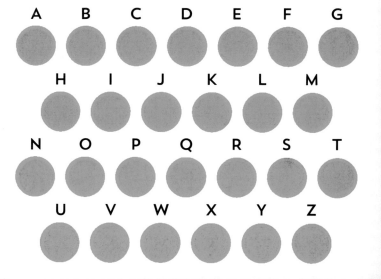

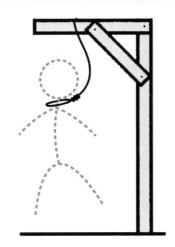

A B C D E F G

H I J K L M

N O P Q R S T

U V W X Y Z

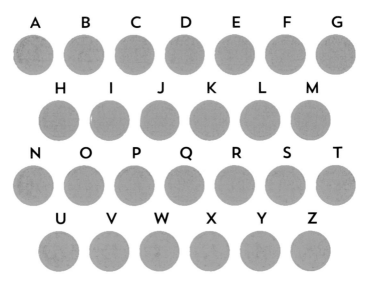

— — — — — — — — — —
1 2 3 4 5 6 7 8 9 10

— — — — —
11 12 13 14 15

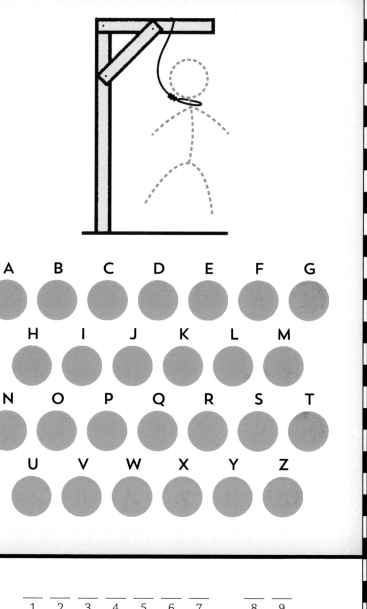

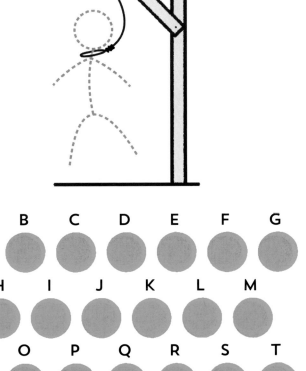

A B C D E F G

H I J K L M

N O P Q R S T

U V W X Y Z

___ ___ ___ ___ ___ ___ ___ ___   ___ ___ ___ ___
1   2   3   4   5   6   7   8   9   10 11 12

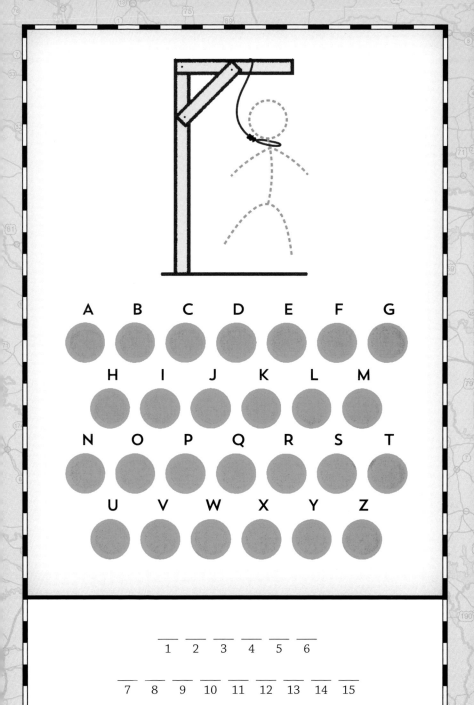

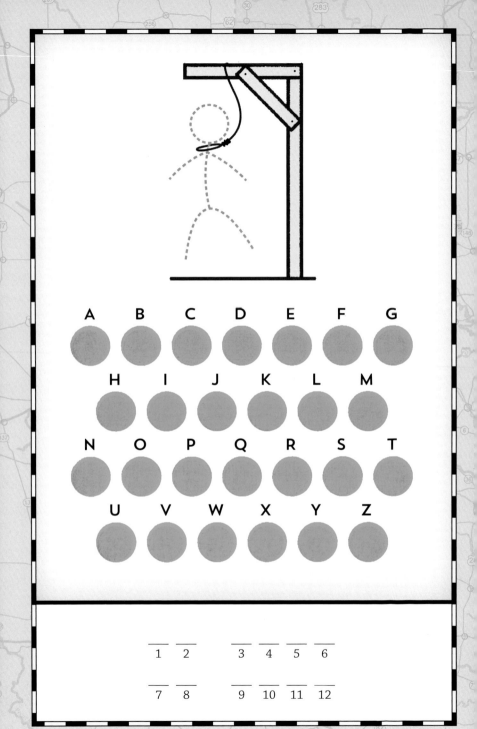

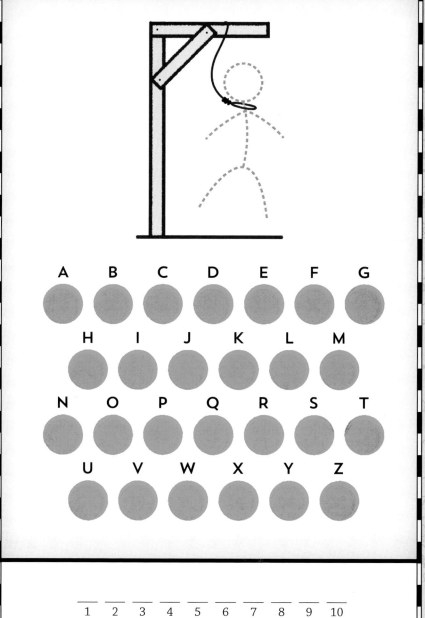

A B C D E F G

H I J K L M

N O P Q R S T

U V W X Y Z

__ __ __ __ __ __ __ __ __ __
1   2   3   4   5   6   7   8   9   10

__ __ __ __ __ __ __ __
11   12   13   14   15   16   17   18

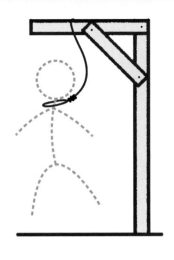

A B C D E F G

H I J K L M

N O P Q R S T

U V W X Y Z

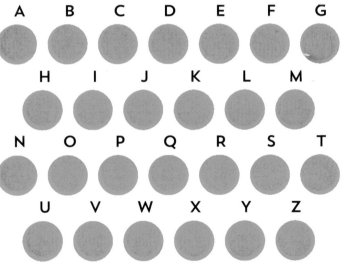

___ ___ ___ ___ ___
1   2   3   4   5

___ ___ ___ ___ ___ ___ ___ ___
6   7   8   9   10 11 12 13

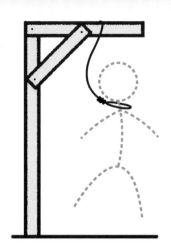

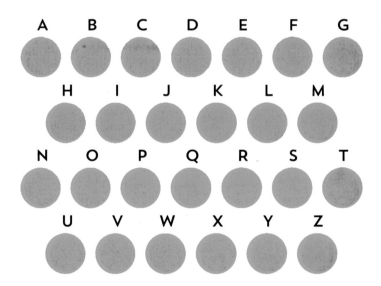

$$\overline{}_{1} \ \overline{}_{2} \ \overline{}_{3} \ \overline{}_{4} \ \overline{}_{5} \ \overline{}_{6} \ \overline{}_{7} \ \overline{}$$

$$\overline{}_{8} \ \overline{}_{9} \ \overline{}_{10} \ \overline{} \ \overline{}_{11} \ \overline{}_{12} \ \overline{}_{13} \ \overline{}_{14}$$

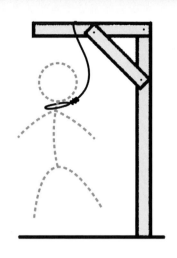

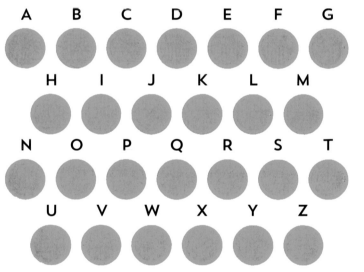

$\overline{}$ $\overline{}$ $\overline{}$ $\overline{}$ $\overline{}$ $\overline{}$ $\overline{}$ $\overline{}$ $\overline{}$
1   2   3   4   5   6   7   8   9

$\overline{}$ $\overline{}$ $\overline{}$ $\overline{}$
10   11   12   13

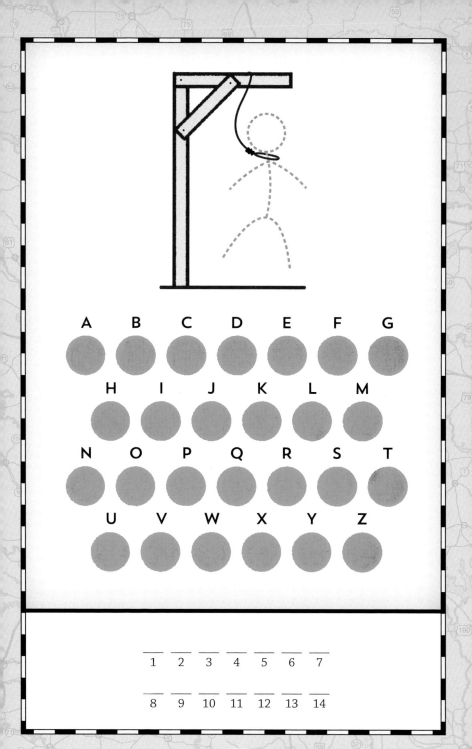

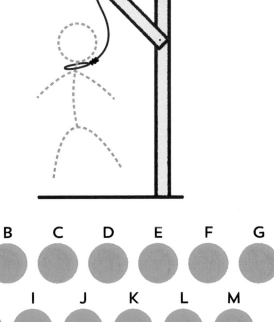

A B C D E F G

H I J K L M

N O P Q R S T

U V W X Y Z

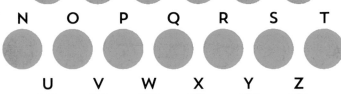

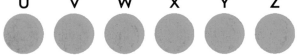

1	2	3	4	5	6	7	8	9	10

11	12	13	14	15	16

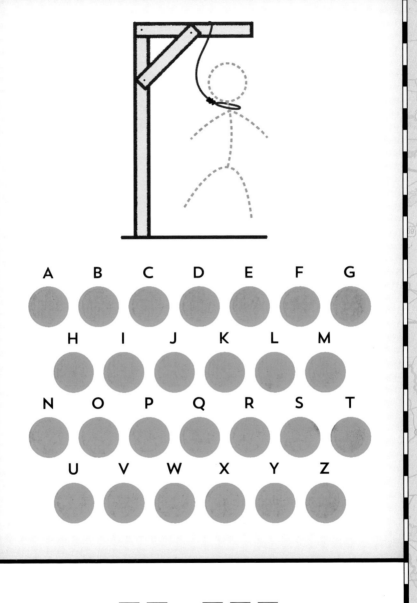

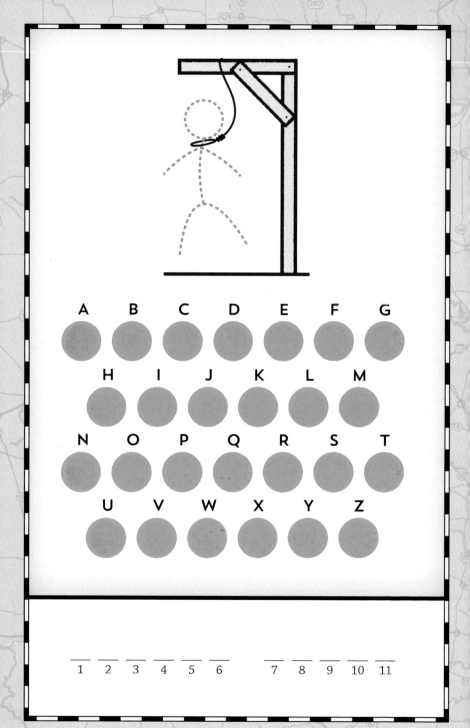

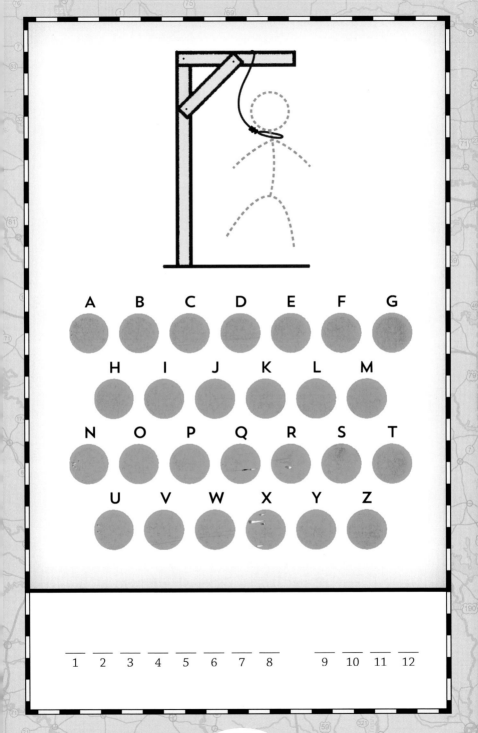

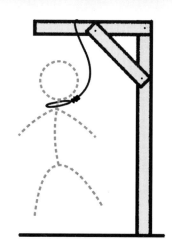

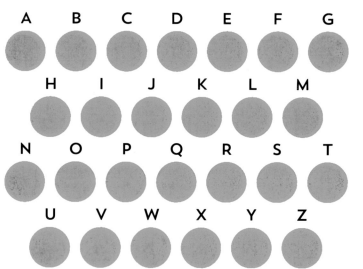

A   B   C   D   E   F   G

H   I   J   K   L   M

N   O   P   Q   R   S   T

U   V   W   X   Y   Z

___ ___ ___ ___ ___ ___
1   2   3   4   5   6

___ ___ ___ ___ ___ ___ ___ ___
7   8   9   10   11   12   13   14

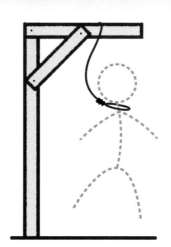

A　B　C　D　E　F　G

H　I　J　K　L　M

N　O　P　Q　R　S　T

U　V　W　X　Y　Z

"
$$\overline{}_{1}\ \overline{}_{2}\ \overline{}_{3}\qquad\overline{}_{4}\ \overline{}_{5}$$

$$\overline{}_{6}\ \overline{}_{7}\ \overline{}_{8}\qquad\overline{}_{9}\ \overline{}_{10}?"$$

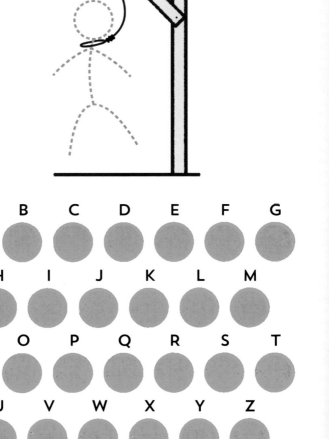

A B C D E F G

H I J K L M

N O P Q R S T

U V W X Y Z

$$\overline{}\ \overline{}\ \overline{}\ \overline{}\ \overline{}\ \overline{}\ \overline{}$$
1   2   3   4   5   6   7

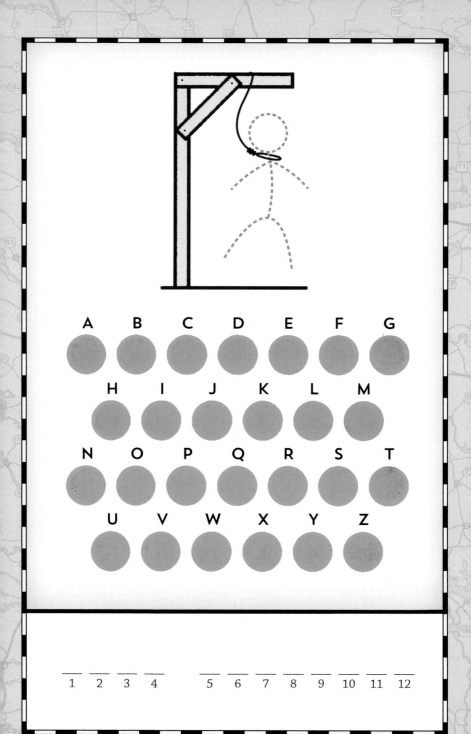

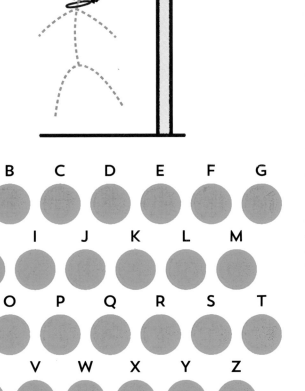

A B C D E F G

H I J K L M

N O P Q R S T

U V W X Y Z

___ ___ ___ ___ ___ ___ ___
1   2   3   4   5   6   7

___ ___ ___ ___ ___ ___ ___
8   9   10 11 12 13 14

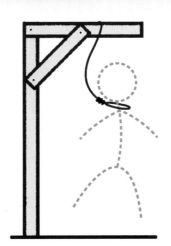

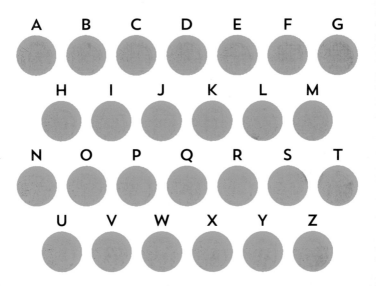

——	——	——	——	——	——	——
1	2	3	4	5	6	7

——	——	——	——	——	——	——
8	9	10	11	12	13	14

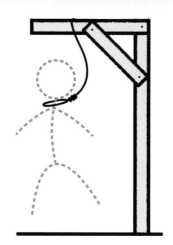

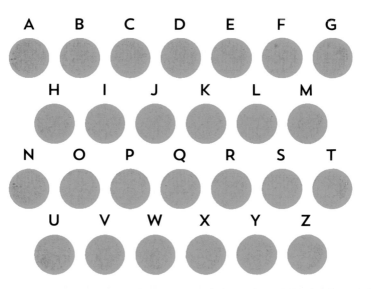

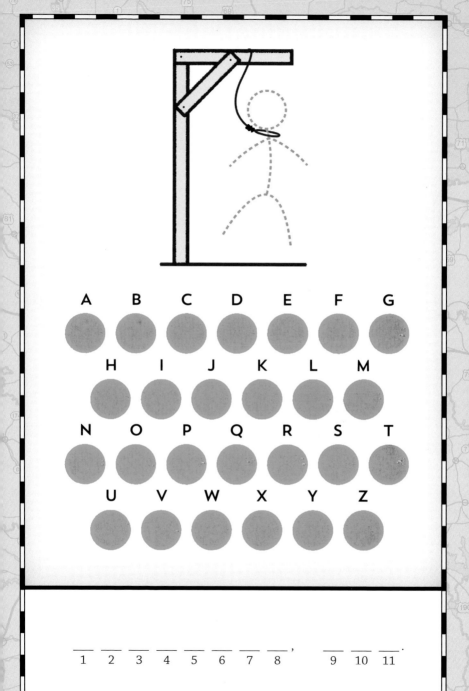

$\overline{}_{1} \ \overline{}_{2} \ \overline{}_{3} \ \overline{}_{4} \ \overline{}_{5} \ \overline{}_{6} \ \overline{}_{7} \ \overline{}_{8} \ , \ \overline{}_{9} \ \overline{}_{10} \ \overline{}_{11} \ .$

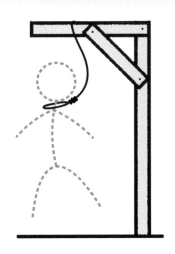

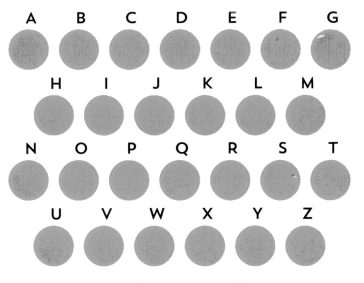

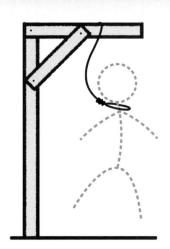

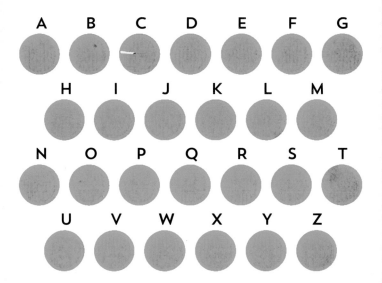

A B C D E F G

H I J K L M

N O P Q R S T

U V W X Y Z

__ __ __ __ __ __
1 2 3 4 5 6

__ __ __ __ __ __ __
7 8 9 10 11 12 13

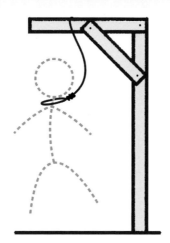

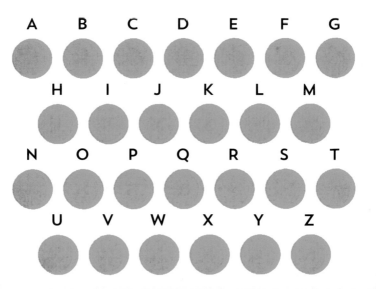

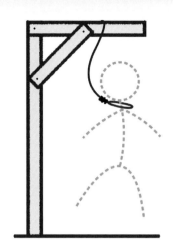

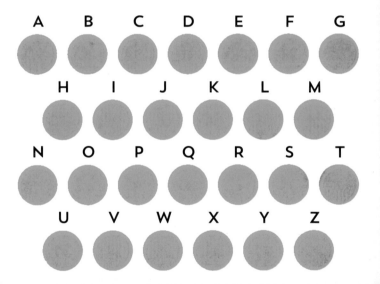

$\overline{}_{1} \overline{}_{2} \overline{}_{3} \overline{}_{4} \overline{}_{5} \overline{}_{6} \overline{}_{7}$,

$\overline{}_{8} \overline{}_{9} \overline{}_{10} \overline{}_{11} \overline{}_{12} \overline{}_{13}$

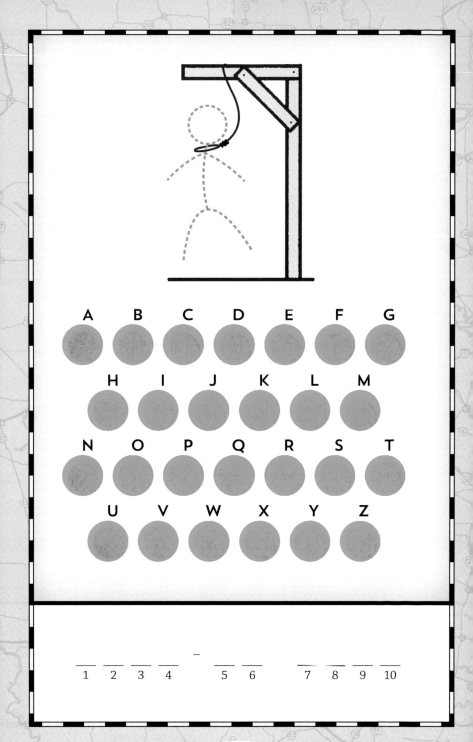

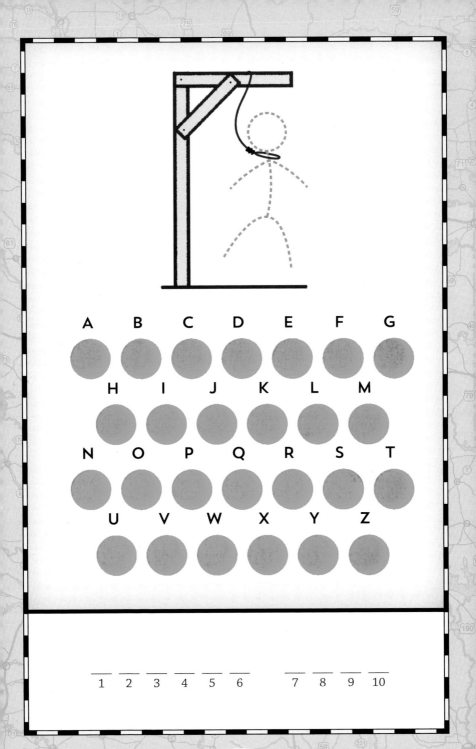

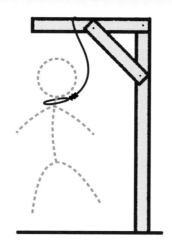

A B C D E F G

H I J K L M

N O P Q R S T

U V W X Y Z

$\overline{}$ $\overline{}$ $\overline{}$ $\overline{}$ $\overline{}$ $\overline{}$ $\overline{}$ $\overline{}$ $\overline{}$ $\overline{}$ $\overline{}$
1   2   3   4   5   6   7   8   9   10   11

$\overline{}$ $\overline{}$ $\overline{}$ $\overline{}$
12   13   14   15

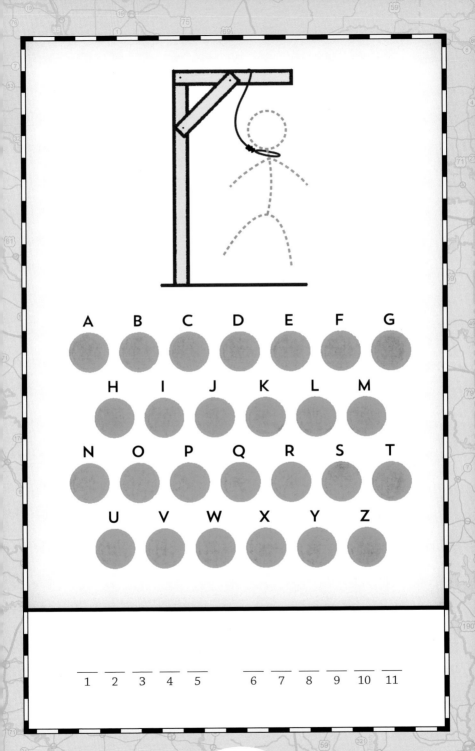

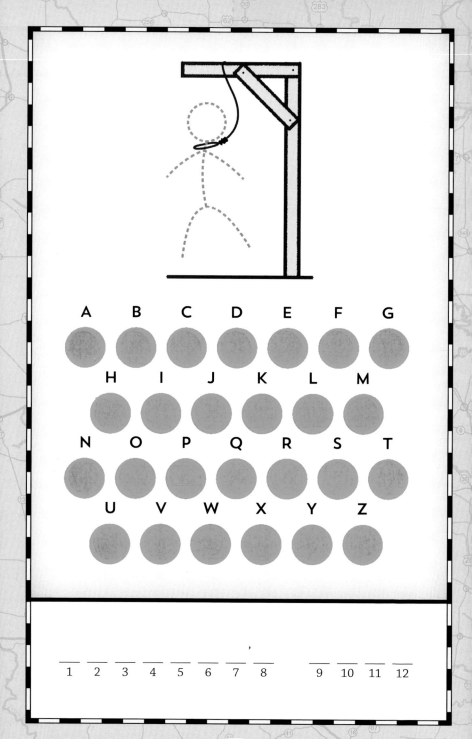

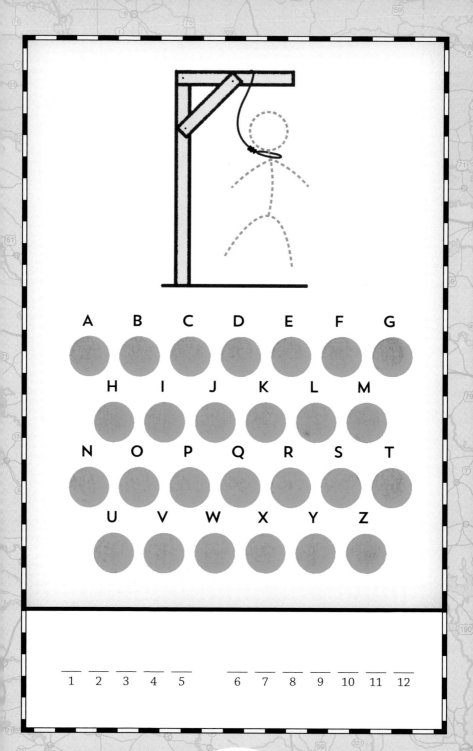

A B C D E F G

H I J K L M

N O P Q R S T

U V W X Y Z

$\overline{}$ $\overline{}$ $\overline{}$ $\overline{}$ $\overline{}$ $\overline{}$ $\overline{}$ $\overline{}$ $\overline{}$ $\overline{}$ $\overline{}$ $\overline{}$
1 2 3 4 5 6 7 8 9 10 11 12

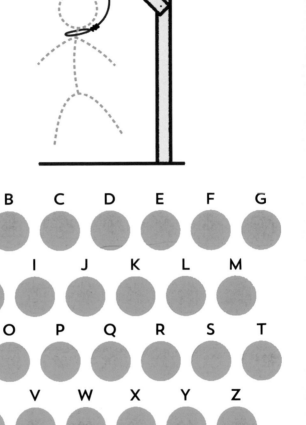

A   B   C   D   E   F   G

H   I   J   K   L   M

N   O   P   Q   R   S   T

U   V   W   X   Y   Z

<u>   </u> <u>   </u> <u>   </u> <u>   </u> <u>   </u> <u>   </u>   <u>   </u> <u>   </u> <u>   </u> <u>   </u> <u>   </u>

 1   2   3   4   5   6   7   8   9   10   11

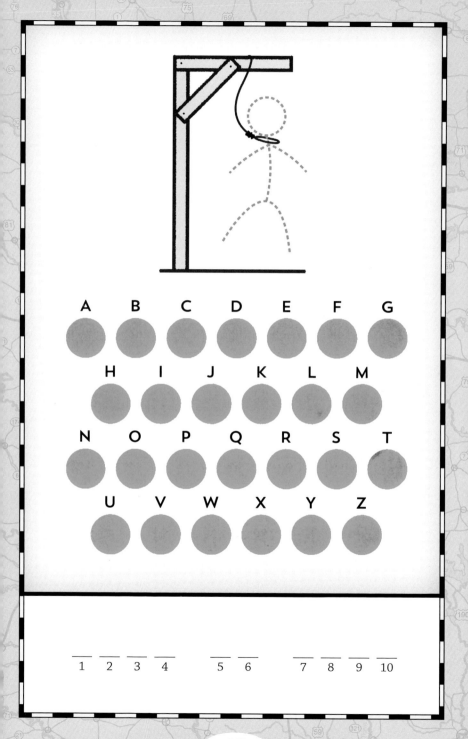

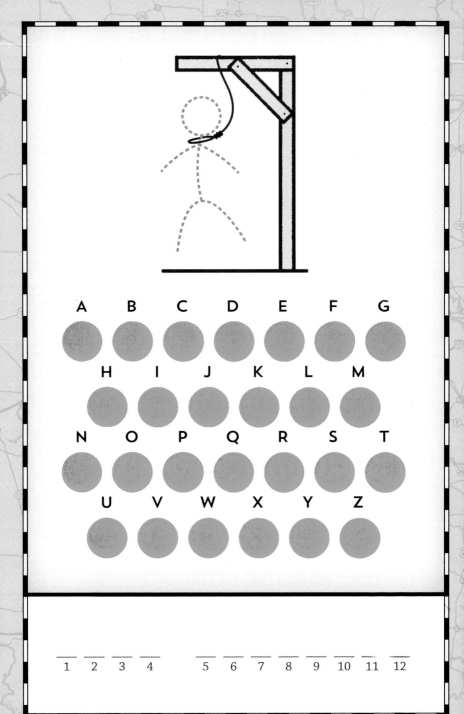

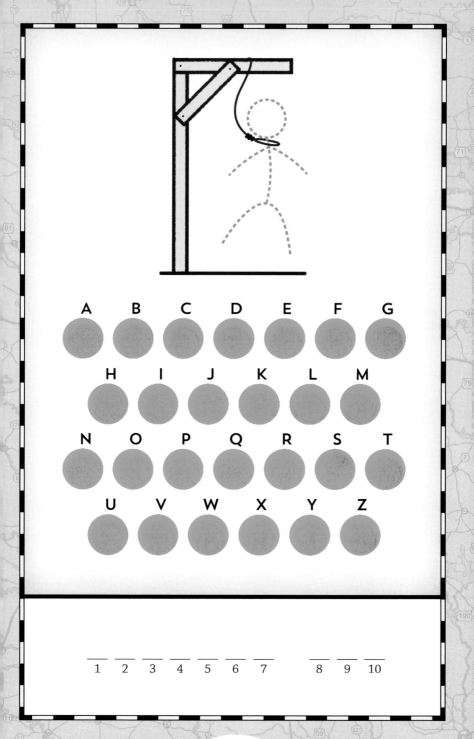

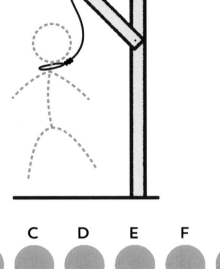

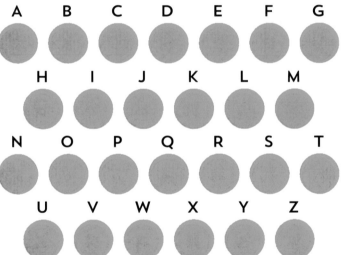

1	2	3	4	5	6	7		8	9	10	11

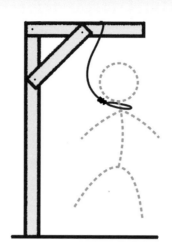

A   B   C   D   E   F   G

H   I   J   K   L   M

N   O   P   Q   R   S   T

U   V   W   X   Y   Z

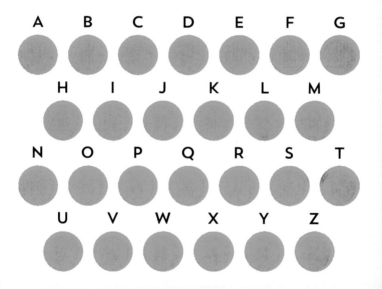

$$\overline{}\ \overline{}\ \overline{}\ \overline{}\ \overline{}\ \overline{}\ \overline{}$$
1   2   3   4   5   6   7

$$\overline{}\ \overline{}\ \overline{}\ \overline{}\ \overline{}\ \overline{}$$
8   9   10   11   12   13

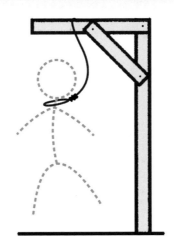

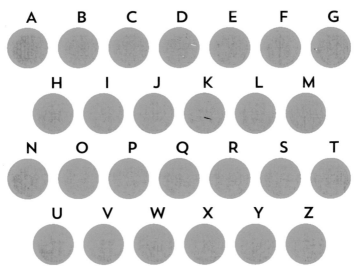

A B C D E F G
H I J K L M
N O P Q R S T
U V W X Y Z

$$\overline{}\ \overline{}\ \overline{}\ \overline{}\ \overline{}\ \overline{}\ \overline{}\ \overline{}\ \overline{}$$
1   2   3   4   5   6   7   8   9

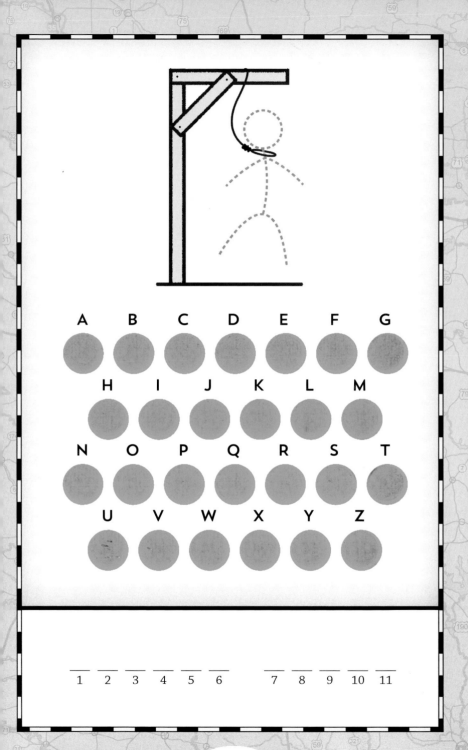

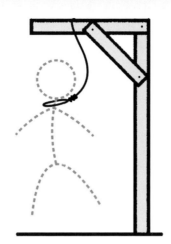

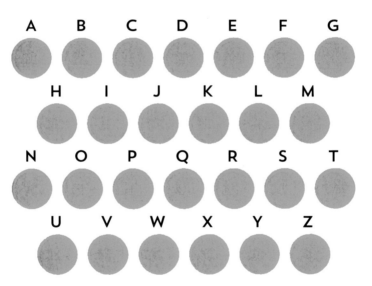

A   B   C   D   E   F   G

H   I   J   K   L   M

N   O   P   Q   R   S   T

U   V   W   X   Y   Z

___ ___ ___ ___ ___ ___ ___
1 2 3 4 5 6 7

___ ___ ___ ___ ___ ___
8 9 10 11 12 13

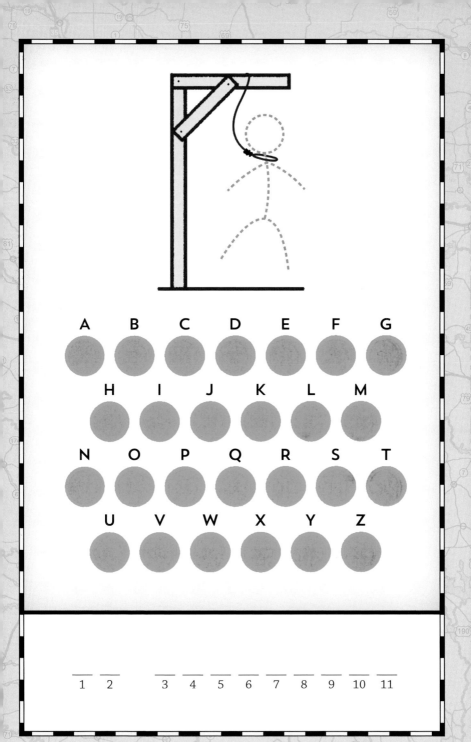

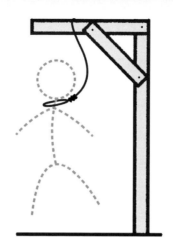

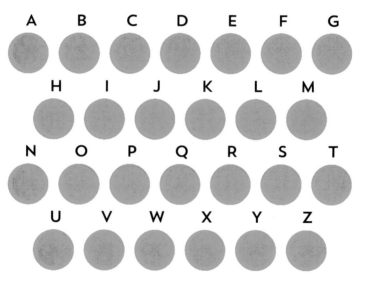

A B C D E F G

H I J K L M

N O P Q R S T

U V W X Y Z

$\overline{}\ \overline{}\ \overline{}\ \overline{}\ \overline{}\ \overline{}\ \overline{}$
1   2   3   4   5   6   7

$\overline{}\ \overline{}\ \overline{}\ \overline{}\ \overline{}\ \overline{}$
8   9   10 11 12 13

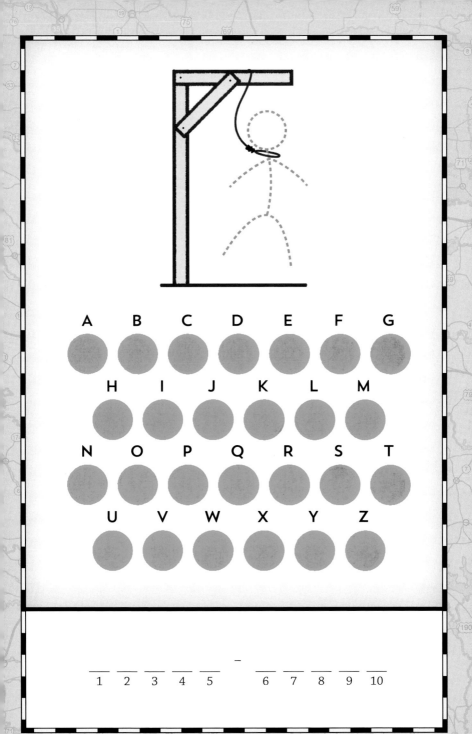

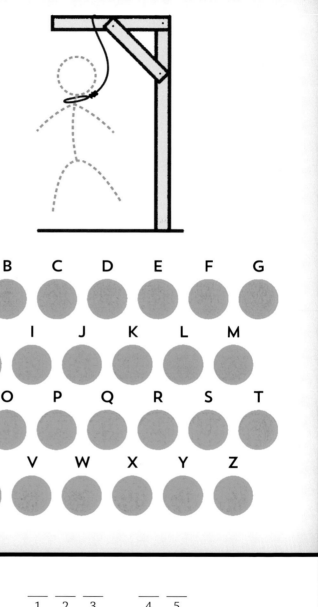

A B C D E F G

H I J K L M

N O P Q R S T

U V W X Y Z

___ ___ ___ ___ ___
1 2 3 4 5

___ ___ ___ ___ ___ ___ ___ ___
6 7 8 9 10 11 12 13

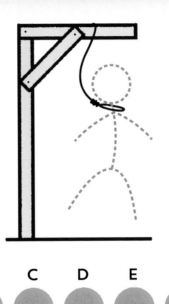

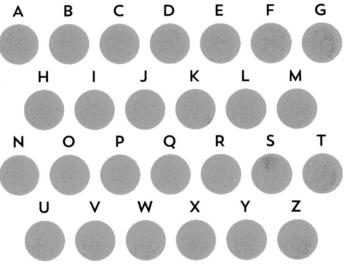

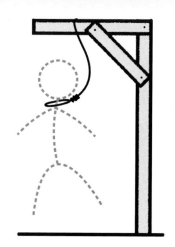

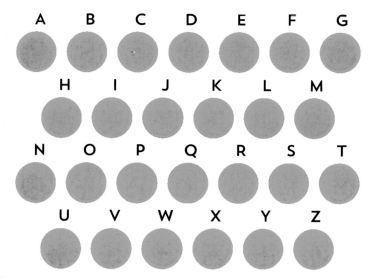

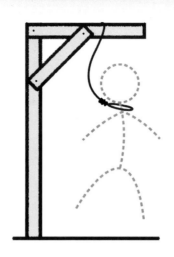

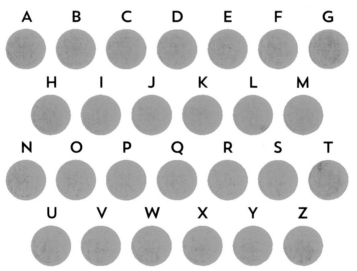

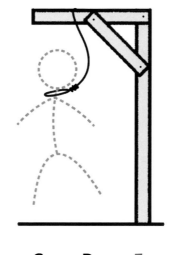

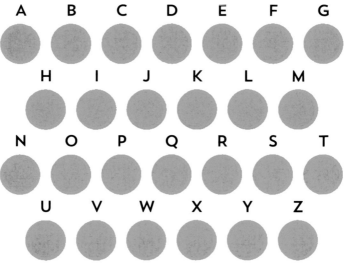

A   B   C   D   E   F   G

H   I   J   K   L   M

N   O   P   Q   R   S   T

U   V   W   X   Y   Z

$\overline{}$ $\overline{}$ $\overline{}$ $\overline{}$ $\overline{}$ $\overline{}$ $\overline{}$ $\overline{}$ $\overline{}$ $\overline{}$ $\overline{}$ $\overline{}$

1   2   3   4   5   6   7   8   9   10   11   12

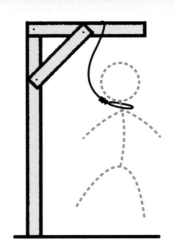

A B C D E F G

H I J K L M

N O P Q R S T

U V W X Y Z

$$\overline{}_{1}\ \overline{}_{2}\ \overline{}_{3}\ \overline{}_{4}\ ,\quad \overline{}_{5}\ \overline{}_{6}\ \overline{}_{7}\ \overline{}_{8}\ ,$$

$$\overline{}_{9}\ \overline{}_{10}\ \overline{}_{11}\ \overline{}_{12}\ \overline{}_{13}$$

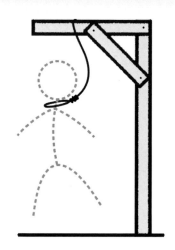

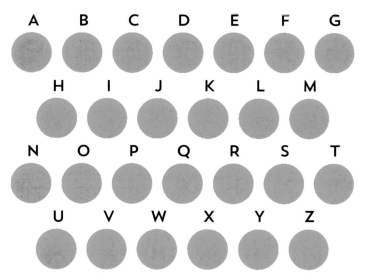

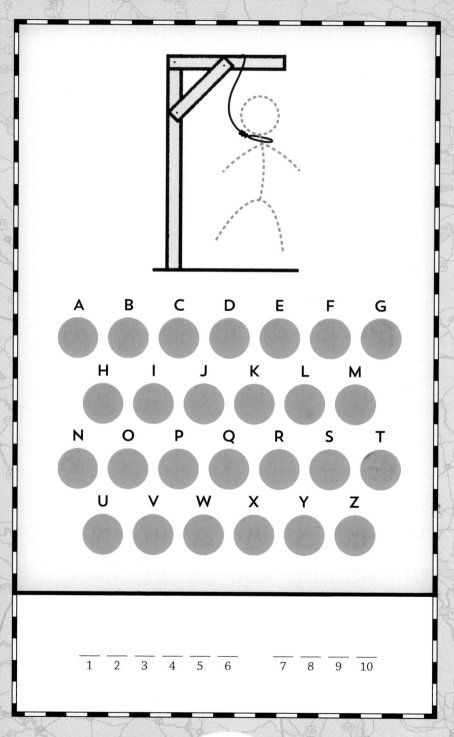

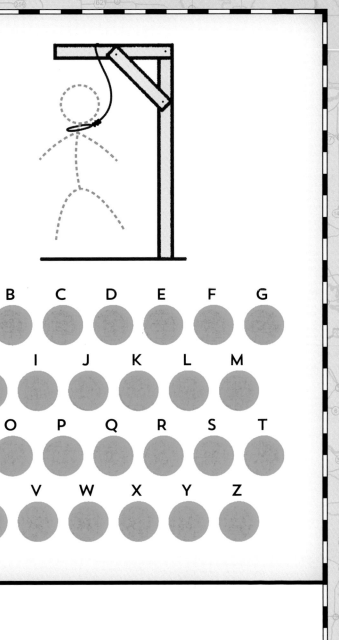

A B C D E F G

H I J K L M

N O P Q R S T

U V W X Y Z

— — — — —   — — — — — — —
1 2 3 4 5   6 7 8 9 10 11 12

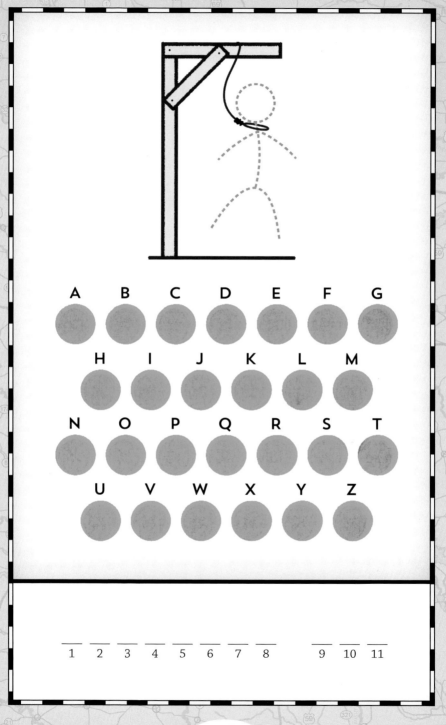

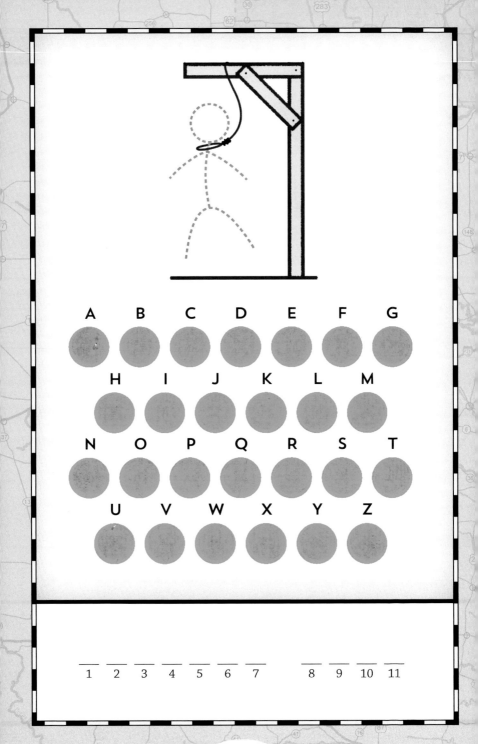

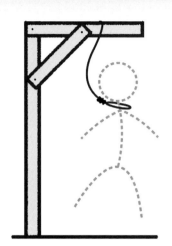

A B C D E F G

H I J K L M

N O P Q R S T

U V W X Y Z

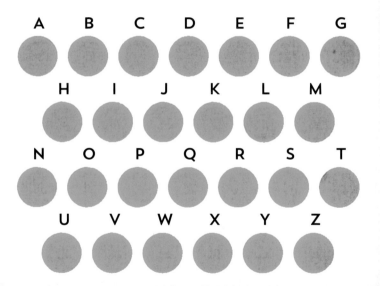

$$\overline{}\ \overline{}\ \overline{}\ \overline{}\qquad \overline{}\ \overline{}\ \overline{}\ \overline{}$$
1 2 3 4   5 6 7 8

$$\overline{}\ \overline{}\ \overline{}\ \overline{}\ \overline{}\ \overline{}$$
9 10 11 12 13 14

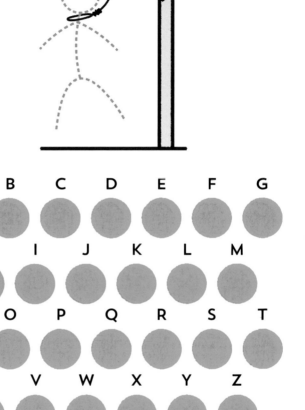

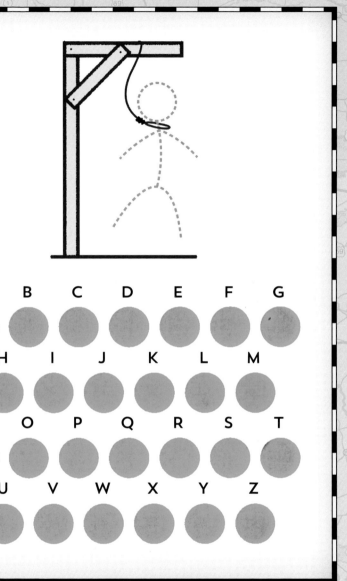

A B C D E F G

H I J K L M

N O P Q R S T

U V W X Y Z

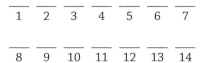

$\overline{}$ $\overline{}$ $\overline{}$ $\overline{}$ $\overline{}$ $\overline{}$ $\overline{}$
1   2   3   4   5   6   7

$\overline{}$ $\overline{}$ $\overline{}$ $\overline{}$ $\overline{}$ $\overline{}$ $\overline{}$
8   9   10   11   12   13   14

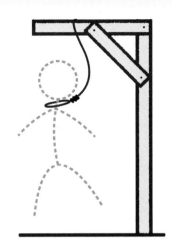

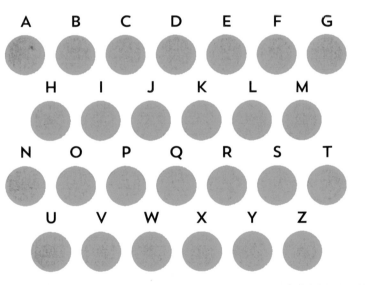

1	2	3	4	5	6	7	8	

9	10	11	12	13

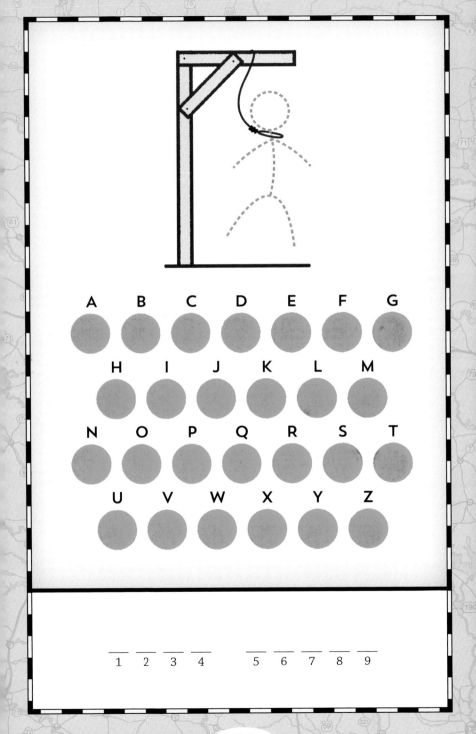

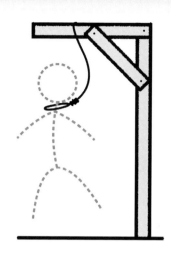

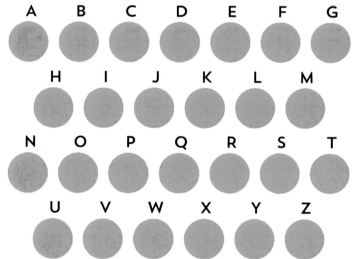

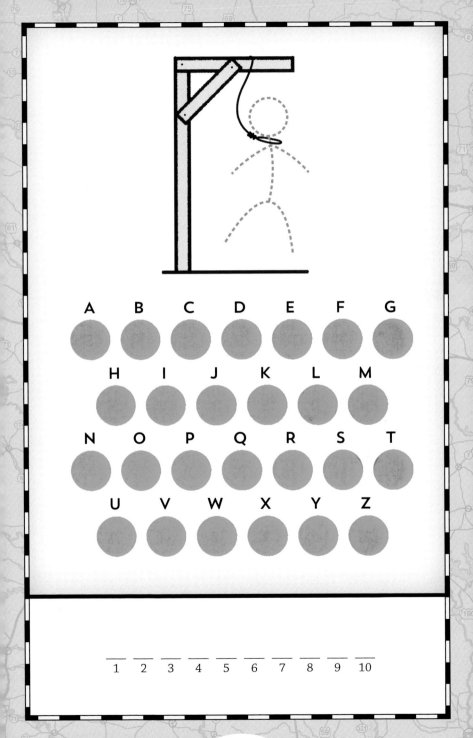

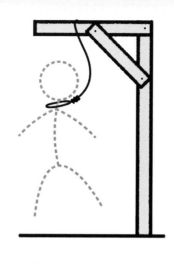

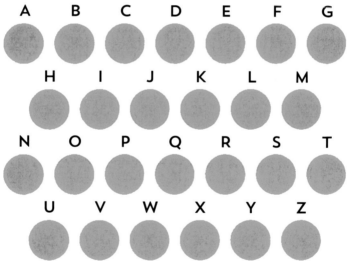

$\overline{}$ $\overline{}$ $\overline{}$ $\overline{}$ $\quad$ $\overline{}$ $\overline{}$ $\overline{}$ $\overline{}$ $\overline{}$ $\overline{}$ $\overline{}$
1 2 3 4   5 6 7 8 9 10 11

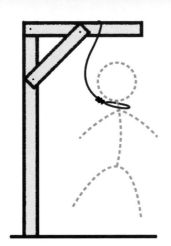

A B C D E F G

H I J K L M

N O P Q R S T

U V W X Y Z

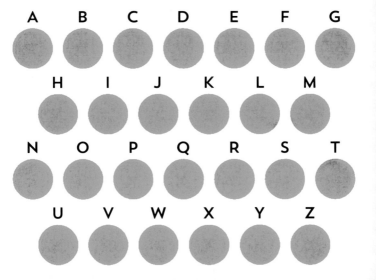

"___ ___ ___ ___ ___ ___ ___
 1   2   3   4   5   6   7

___ ___ ___ ___ ___ ___ ___!"
 8   9 10 11 12 13 14

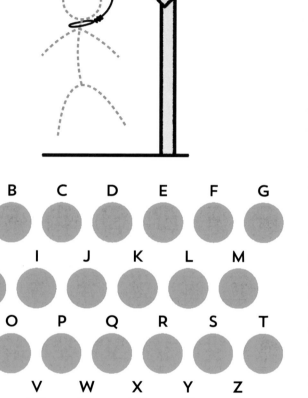

A B C D E F G

H I J K L M

N O P Q R S T

U V W X Y Z

___ ___ ___ ___ ___ ___ ___ ___ ___ ___
1   2   3   4   5   6   7   8   9 10

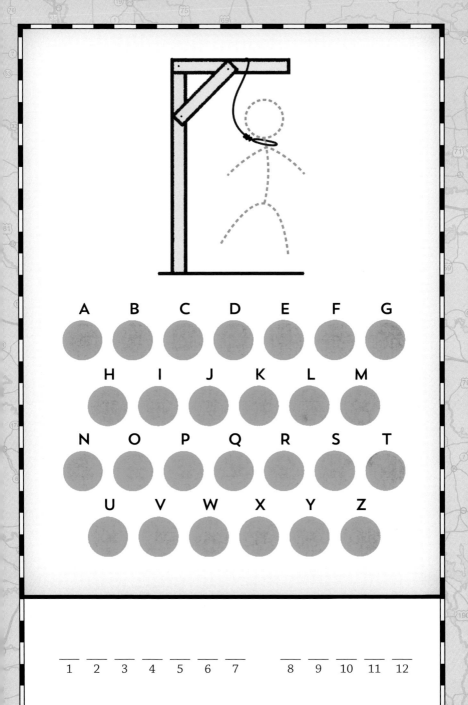

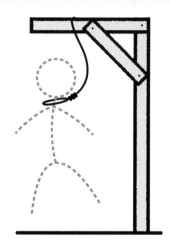

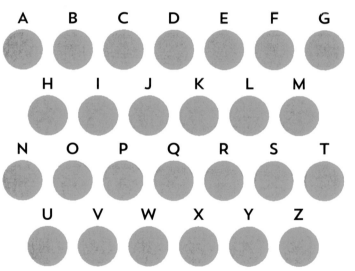

A B C D E F G

H I J K L M

N O P Q R S T

U V W X Y Z

___ ___ ___ ___ ___ ___ ___ ___ ___
1   2   3   4   5   6   7   8   9

___ ___ ___ ___ ___
10 11 12 13 14

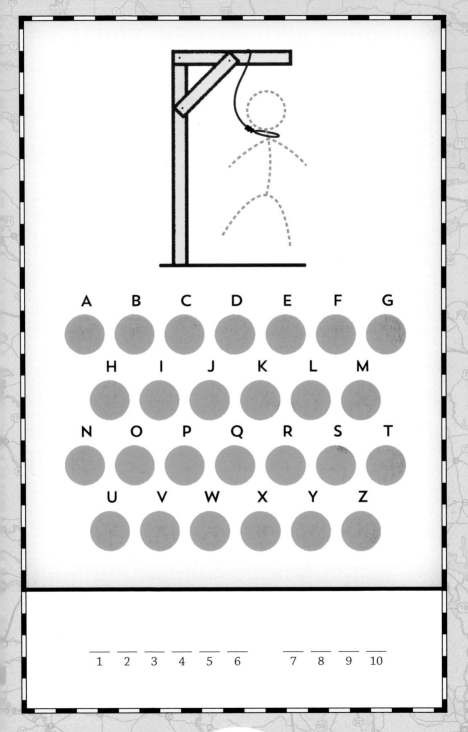

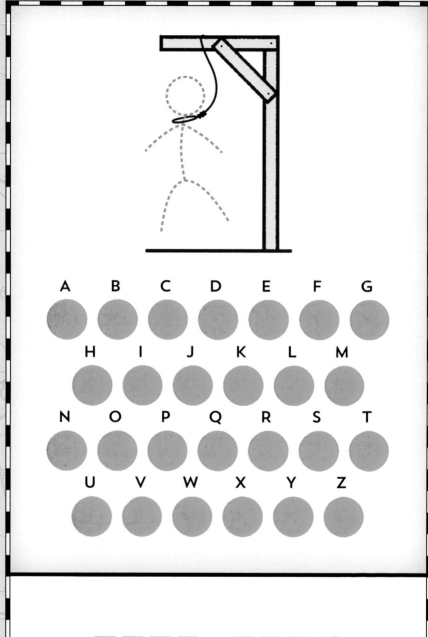

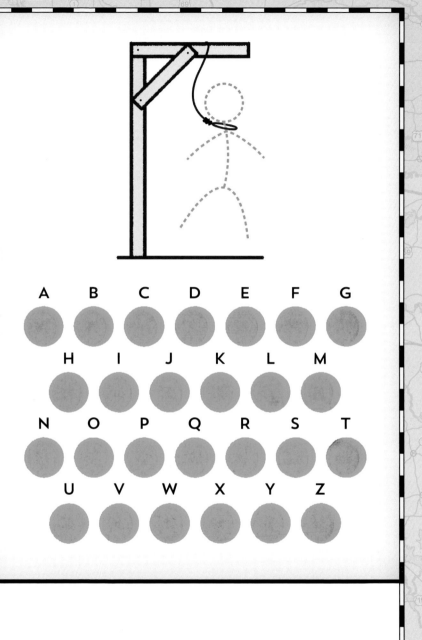

A B C D E F G

H I J K L M

N O P Q R S T

U V W X Y Z

___ ___ ___ ___ ___ ___   ___ ___ ___ ___ ___ ___
1   2   3   4   5   6   7   8   9   10 11 12

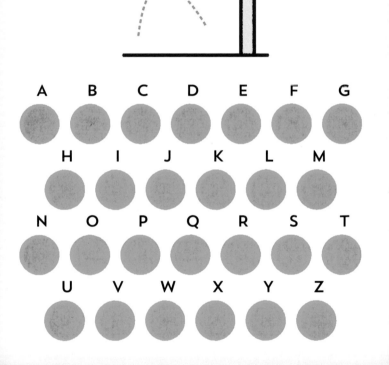

A B C D E F G

H I J K L M

N O P Q R S T

U V W X Y Z

___ ___ ___ ___ ___   ___ ___ ___
1   2   3   4   5   6   7   8

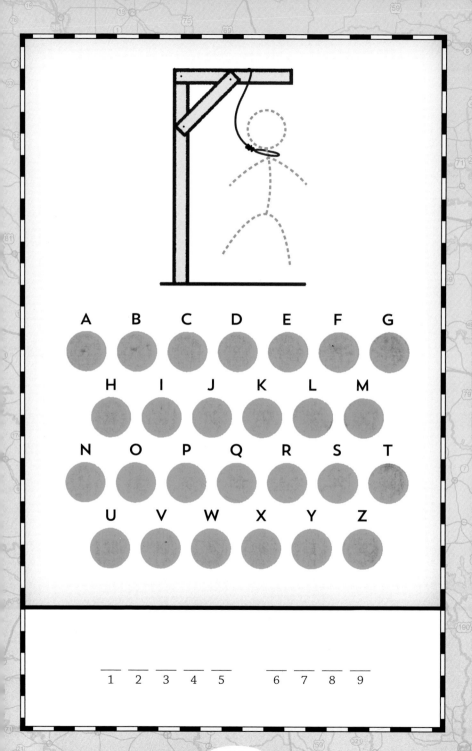

A B C D E F G

H I J K L M

N O P Q R S T

U V W X Y Z

___ ___ ___ ___ ___   ___ ___ ___ ___
 1   2   3   4   5   6   7   8   9

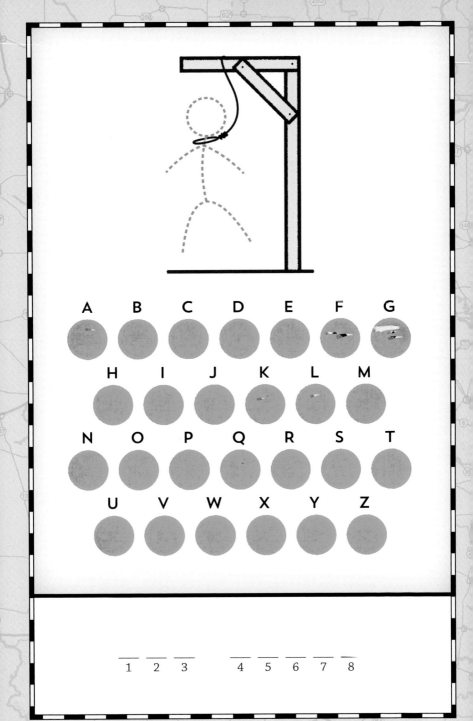

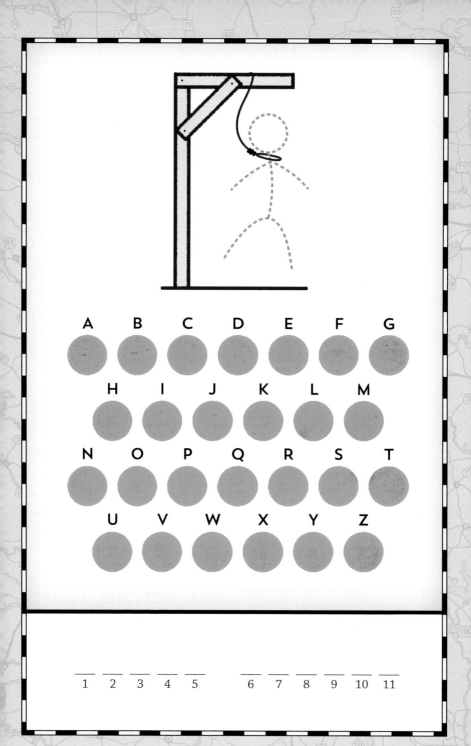

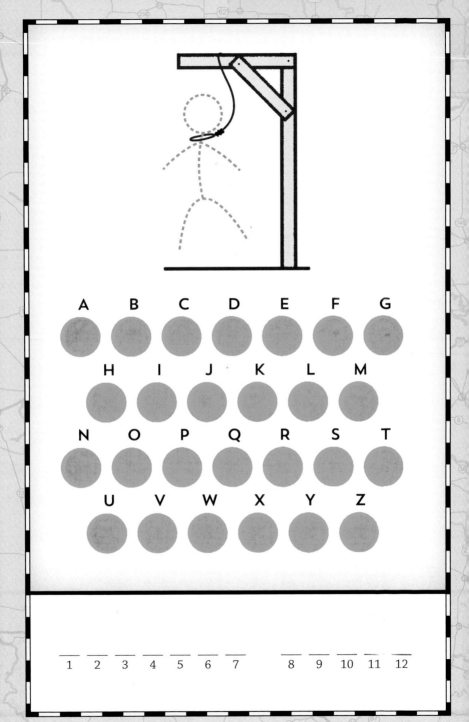

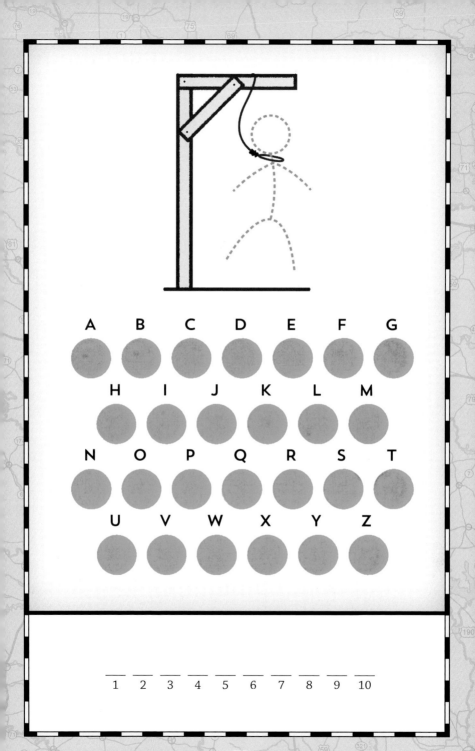

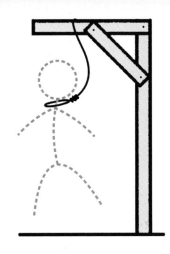

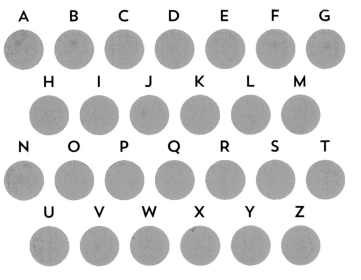

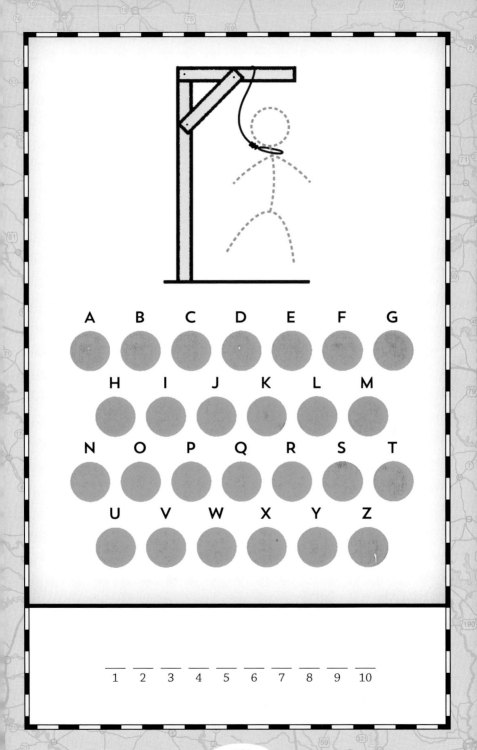

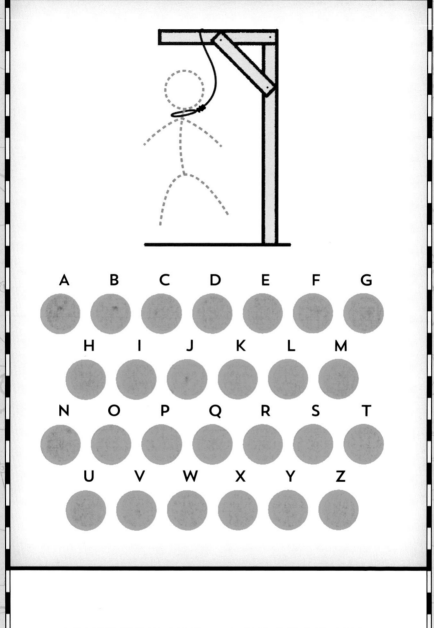

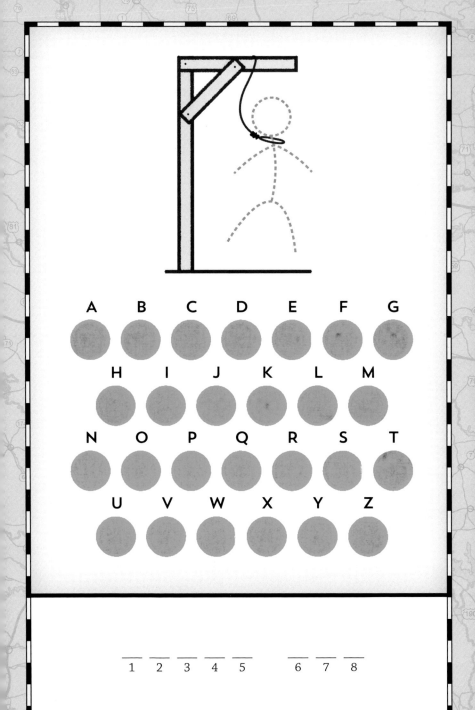

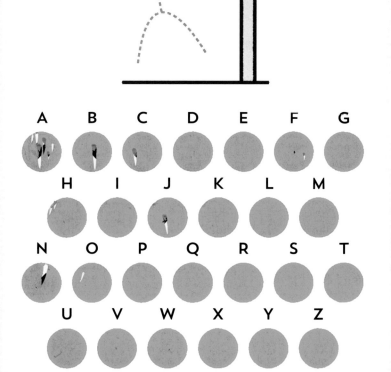

A   B   C   D   E   F   G

H   I   J   K   L   M

N   O   P   Q   R   S   T

U   V   W   X   Y   Z

___ ___ ___ ___ ___ ___ ___ ___ ___
1   2   3   4   5   6   7   8   9

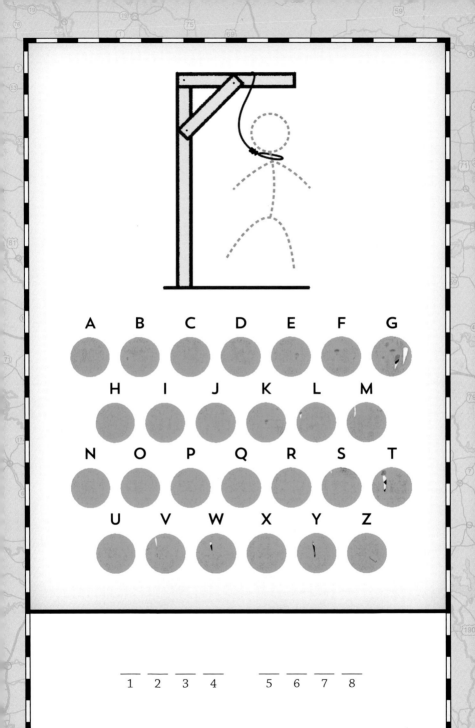

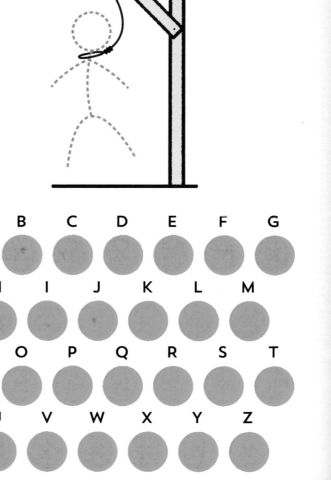

A B C D E F G

H I J K L M

N O P Q R S T

U V W X Y Z

<u> </u> <u> </u> <u> </u> <u> </u>   <u> </u> <u> </u> <u> </u> <u> </u> <u> </u> <u> </u>
1 2 3 4   5 6 7 8 9 10

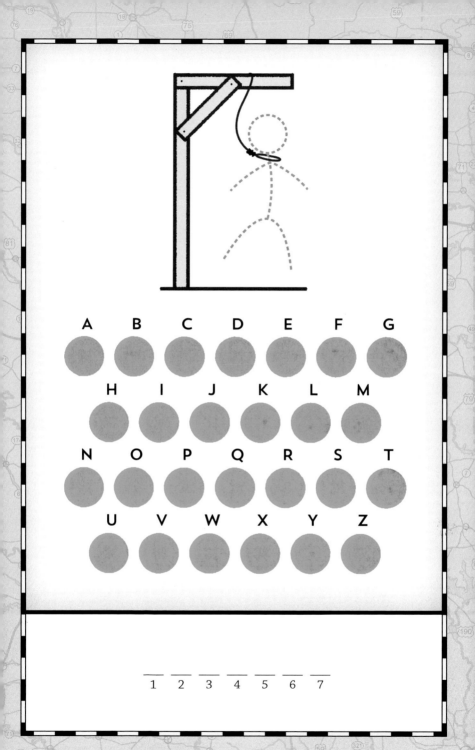

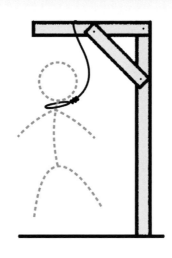

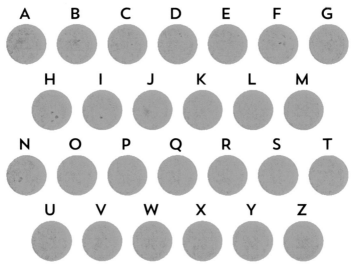

A B C D E F G

H I J K L M

N O P Q R S T

U V W X Y Z

‾ ‾ ‾ ‾ ‾ ‾ ‾ ‾ ‾
1 2 3 4 5 6 7 8 9

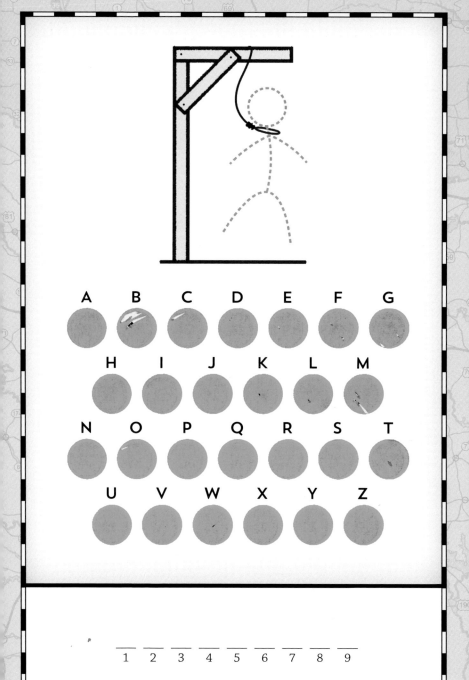

A B C D E F G
H I J K L M
N O P Q R S T
U V W X Y Z

___ ___ ___ ___ ___ ___ ___ ___ ___
1   2   3   4   5   6   7   8   9

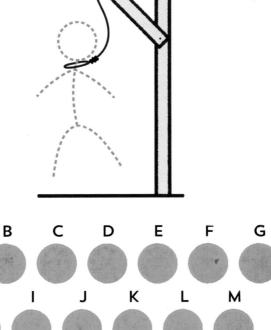

A B C D E F G

H I J K L M

N O P Q R S T

U V W X Y Z

$$\frac{\quad}{1} \frac{\quad}{2} \frac{\quad}{3} \frac{\quad}{4} \frac{\quad}{5} \frac{\quad}{6} \frac{\quad}{7} \frac{\quad}{8} \frac{\quad}{9}$$